# How to Pray

## R. A. Torrey

## Publisher's Note

*HOW TO PRAY is a classic teaching on prayer by a mighty man of God, R.A. Torrey. This updated, contemporized edition flows with the same message and intent of the original nineteenth century version. May God bless all who read this book.*

## HOW TO PRAY

Copyright © 1983 by Whitaker House
Printed in the United States of America
ISBN: 0-88368-133-1

# CONTENTS

Chapter 1

# THE IMPORTANCE OF PRAYER

In Ephesians 6:18, the tremendous importance of prayer is expressed with startling and over-whelming force:

"Praying always with all prayer and supplication in the Spirit, and watching thereunto with all perseverance and supplication for all saints."

When the perceptive child of God stops to weigh the meaning of these words then notes the connection in which they are found, he or she is driven to say, "I must pray, pray, pray. I must put all my energy and heart into prayer. Whatever else I do, I must pray."

The Revised Standard Version is sometimes even more emphatic than the King James:

"Pray at all times in the Spirit, with all prayer and supplication. To that end keep alert with all perseverance, making supplication for all the saints."

Notice the *alls:* "Pray at *all* times," "with *all* prayer," "in *all* perseverance," "for *all* the saints." Note the piling up of strong words, "prayer," "supplication," "perseverance." Also notice the strong expression, "to that end keep alert," more literally, "in this, be not lazy." Paul realized the natural apathy of man, and especially his natural neglect in prayer. How seldom we pray things through! How often the Church and the individual get right up to the verge of a great blessing in prayer and then let go, become lazy, and quit. I wish that these words "in this, be not lazy" might burn into our heart. I wish the whole verse would burn into our heart.

### The Necessity Of Persistent Prayer

Why is this constant, persistent, sleepless, overcoming prayer so necessary?

*Because there is a devil.*

He is cunning; he is mighty; he never rests; he is continually plotting the downfall of the child of God. If the child of God relaxes in prayer, the devil will succeed in ensnaring him.

This is the meaning of the text. Ephesians 6:12 reads: "For we wrestle not against flesh and blood, but against principalities, against powers, against rulers of the darkness of this world, against spiritual wickedness in high places." Then comes Ephesians 6:13: "Wherefore take unto you the whole armour of God, that ye may be able to withstand in the evil day, and having done all, to stand." Next follows a description of the different parts of the Christian's armor which we are to put on if we are to stand against Satan and his mighty wiles. Paul brings all to a climax in Ephesians

6:18, telling us that to all else we must add prayer—constant, persistent, untiring, sleepless prayer in the Holy Spirit—or all else will be in vain.

*Prayer is God's appointed way for obtaining things. The reason we lack anything in life is due to neglect of prayer.*

James points this out very forcibly in chapter 4, verse 2, of his epistle: "Ye have not, because ye ask not." These words contain the secret of the poverty and powerlessness of the average Christian—neglect of prayer.

Many Christians are asking, "Why is it that I progress so little in my Christian life?"

"Neglect of prayer," God answers. "You have not, because you ask not."

Many ministers are asking, "Why is it I see so little fruit from my labors?"

Again, God answers, "Neglect of prayer. You have not, because you ask not."

Many Sunday school teachers are asking, "Why is it that I see so few converted in my Sunday school class?"

Still, God answers, "Neglect of prayer. You have not, because you ask not."

Both ministers and churches are asking, "Why is it that the Church of Christ makes so little headway against unbelief and error and sin and worldliness?"

Once more, we hear God answering, "Neglect of prayer. You have not, because you ask not."

*Those men whom God set forth as a pattern of*

*what He expected Christians to be—the apostles—regarded prayer as the most important business of their lives.*

When the multiplying responsibilities of the early Church crowded in upon them, they "called the multitude of the disciples unto them, and said, It is not reason that we should leave the Word of God, and serve tables. Wherefore, brethren, look ye out among you seven men of honest report, full of the Holy Ghost and wisdom, whom we may appoint over this business. But *we will give ourselves continually to prayer,* and to the ministry of the Word" (Acts 6:2-4). It is evident, from what Paul wrote to both churches and individuals, that much of his time and strength and thought were devoted to prayer for them. (See Romans 119; Ephesians 1:15,16; Colossians 1:9; 1 Thessalonians 3:10; 2 Timothy 1:3).

All the mighty men of God outside the Bible have been men of prayer. They have differed from one another in many things, but in this they have been alike.

### The Ministry Of Intercession

*Prayer occupied a very prominent place and played a very important part in the earthly life of our Lord.*

Turn, for example, to Mark 1:35. "And in the morning, rising up a great while before day, He went out, and departed into a solitary place, and there prayed." The preceding day had been a very busy and exciting one, but Jesus shortened the

8

hours of needed sleep so that He could rise early and give Himself to more sorely needed prayer.

Turn again to Luke 6:12, where we read, "And it came to pass in those days, that He went out into a mountain to pray, and continued all night in prayer to God." Our Savior occasionally found it necessary to spend a whole night in prayer.

The words *pray* and *prayer* are used at least twenty-five times in connection with our Lord in the brief record of his life in the four gospels, and His praying is mentioned in places where the words are not used. Evidently prayer took much of Jesus' time and strength. A man or woman who does not spend much time in prayer cannot properly be called a follower of Jesus Christ.

*Praying is the most important part of the present ministry of our risen Lord.* This reason for constant, persistent, sleepless, overcoming prayer seems, if possible, even more forcible than the others.

Christ's ministry did not close with His death. His atoning work was finished then. But, when He rose and ascended to the right hand of the Father, He entered into other work for us, work just as important in its place as His atoning work. It cannot be separated from His atoning work because it rests upon that as its basis and is necessary to our complete salvation.

We read what that great present work is, by which He carries our salvation on to completeness, in Hebrews 7:25: "Wherefore He is able also to save them to the uttermost that come unto God by Him, seeing *He ever liveth to make intercession for them."* This verse tells us that Jesus is able to save us unto the uttermost, not merely *from* the uttermost, but *unto* the uttermost—unto entire completeness, absolute perfection. He is able to do this not only because He died, but because He also "ever liveth."

The verse also tells us why He now lives, *"to make intercession for us,"* to pray. Praying is the principal thing He is doing in these days. It is by His prayers that He is saving us.

The same thought is found in Paul's remarkable, triumphant challenge in Romans 8:34: "Who is he that condemneth? It is Christ that died, yea rather, that is risen again, who is even at the right hand of God, *who also maketh intercession for us."*

If we are to then have fellowship with Jesus Christ in His present work, we must spend much time in prayer. We must give ourselves to earnest, constant, persistent, sleepless, overcoming prayer. I know of nothing that has so impressed me with a sense of the importance of praying at all seasons— being much and constantly in prayer—as the thought that this is the principal occupation of my risen Lord even now. I want to have fellowship with Him. For that reason I have asked the Father, whatever else He may make me, to make me at all events an intercessor. I pray He will make me a man who knows how to pray and who spends much time in prayer.

This ministry of intercession is glorious and mighty, and we can all have a part in it. The man or woman who cannot attend the prayer meeting because of illness can have a part in it. The busy mother and the woman who works outside the home can have a part. They can mingle prayers for the saints, for their pastor, for the unsaved, and for foreign missionaries with their day's work. The hard-driven man of business can have a part in it, praying as he hurries from duty to duty. But we must, if we want to maintain this spirit of constant prayer, take time—and plenty of it—when we shut ourselves up in the secret place alone with God for nothing but prayer.

### Receiving Mercy, Grace And Joy

*Prayer is the means that God has appointed for our receiving mercy and obtaining grace to help in time of need.*

Hebrews 4:16 is one of the simplest and sweetest verses in the Bible. "Let us therefore come boldly unto the throne of grace, that we may obtain mercy, and find grace to help in time of need." These words make it very clear that God has appointed a way by which we can seek and obtain mercy and grace. That way is prayer; bold, confident, outspoken approach to the throne of grace, the most holy place of God's presence. There our sympathizing High Priest, Jesus Christ, has entered in our behalf. (See Hebrews 4:14-15.)

Mercy is what we need and grace is what we must have or else all our life and effort will end in complete failure. Prayer is the way to obtain mercy and grace. There is infinite grace at our disposal, and we make it ours by prayer. Oh, if we only realized the fullness of God's grace which is ours for the asking—its height and depth and length and breadth—I am sure we would spend more time in prayer. The measure of our appropriation of grace is determined by the measure of our prayers.

Who does not feel that he needs more grace? Then, ask for it. Be constant and persistent in your asking. Be diligent and untiring in your asking. God delights to have us "shameless" beggars in prayer; for it shows our faith in Him, and He is mightily pleased with faith. Because of our "shamelessness," He will rise and give us as much as we need (see Luke 11:8). What little streams of mercy and grace most of us know, when we might know rivers overflowing their banks!

*Prayer in the name of Jesus Christ is the way He Himself has appointed for His disciples to obtain fullness of joy.*

He states this simply and beautifully in John 16:24: "Hitherto have ye asked nothing in My name; ask, and ye shall receive, that your joy may be full." Who does not wish for full joy? Well, the way to have full joy is by praying in the name of Jesus. We all know people who are full of joy. Indeed, it is just running over, shining from their eyes, bubbling out of their very lips, and running off their fingertips when they shake your hand. Coming in contact with them is like coming in contact with with an electrical machine charged with gladness. People of that sort are always peo-

12

ple who spend much time in prayer.

Why is it that prayer in the name of Christ brings such fullness of joy? In part, because we get what we ask. But, that is not the only reason, nor is it the greatest. It makes God real. When we ask something definite of God, and He gives it, how real God becomes! He is right there! It is blessed to have a God who is real and not merely an idea. I remember once when I suddenly and seriously fell ill all alone in my study. I dropped upon my knees and cried to God for help. Instantly, all pain left me—I was perfectly well. It seemed as if God stood right there and had put out His hand and touched me. The joy of the healing was not as great as the joy of meeting God.

There is no greater joy on earth or in heaven than communion with God. Prayer in the name of Jesus brings us into communion with God. The Psalmist was surely not speaking only of future blessedness, but also of present blessedness, when he said, "In Thy presence is fullness of joy" (Psalm 16:11). Oh, the unutterable joy of those moments when, in our prayers, we really enter into the presence of God!

Does someone say, "I have never known any such joy as that in prayer"? Do you take enough leisure for prayer to actually get into God's presence? Do you really give yourself up to prayer in the time which you do take?

### Freedom From Anxiety

*Prayer with thanksgiving, in every care and*

13

*anxiety and need of life, is the means that God has appointed for our obtaining freedom from all anxiety and the peace of God which passes all understanding.*

"Be careful for nothing," says Paul, "but in every thing by prayer and supplication with thanksgiving let your requests be made known unto God. And the peace of God, which passeth all understanding, shall keep your hearts and minds through Christ Jesus" (Philippians 4:6-7). To many this initially seems like the picture of a life that is beautiful but beyond the reach of ordinary mortals. This is not so at all. The verse tells us how this life of peace is attainable by every child of God: "Be careful for nothing," or as the Revised Standard Version reads, "Have no anxiety about anything." The remainder of the verse tells us how to do this. It is very simple: "But in every thing by prayer and supplication with thanksgiving let your requests be made known unto God." What could be plainer or more simple than that? Just keep in constant touch with God. When trouble or vexation, great or small, occur, speak to Him about it, never forgetting to return thanks for what He has already done. What will the result be? "The peace of God, which passeth all understanding, will keep your hearts and your minds in Christ Jesus" (R.S.V.).

That is glorious, and it is as simple as it is glorious! Thank God, many are trying it. Don't you know anyone who is always serene? Perhaps he is a very stormy man by nature. Troubles and conflicts

14

and opposition and sorrow may sweep around him, and the peace of God which passes all understanding will guard his heart and his thoughts in Christ Jesus.

We all know such persons. How do they do it?

Just by prayer, that is all. Those persons who know the deep peace of God, the unfathomable peace which passes all understanding, are always men and women of much prayer.

Some of us let the hurry of our lives crowd prayer out, and what a waste of time and energy and emotion there is in this constant worry! One night of prayer will save us from many nights of insomnia. Time spent in prayer is not wasted, but time invested at big interest.

### Vehicle For The Holy Spirit

*Prayer is the method that God Himself has appointed for our obtaining the Holy Spirit.*

The Bible is very plain on this point. Jesus says, "If ye then, being evil, know how to give good gifts unto your children: how much more shall your heavenly Father give the Holy Spirit to them that ask Him?" (Luke 11:13).

I know this as definitely as I know that my thirst is quenched when I drink water. Early one morning in the Chicago Avenue Church prayer room, where several hundred people had been assembled a number of hours in prayer, the Holy Spirit fell so manifestly that no one could speak or pray. The whole place was so filled with His presence that sobs of joy filled the place. Men left that room

15

and went to different parts of the country, taking trains that very morning, and the effects of the outpouring of God's Holy Spirit in answer to prayer were soon reported. Others went out into the city with the blessing of God upon them. This is only one instance among many that might be cited from personal experience.

If we would only spend more time in prayer, there would be more fullness of the Spirit's power in our work. Many men who once worked unmistakably in the power of the Holy Spirit now fill the air with empty shoutings, beat it with meaningless gestures, because they have neglected prayer. We must spend much time on our knees before God if we are to continue in the power of the Holy Spirit.

### Be Ready For His Return

*Prayer is the means that Christ has appointed so that our hearts will not be overcome with indulgence and drunkenness and the cares of this life. For, the day of Christ's return will come upon us suddenly as a snare.*

One of the most interesting and solemn passages on prayer in the Bible is along this line (Luke 21:34-36). "Take heed to yourselves, lest at any time your hearts be overcharged with surfeiting and drunkenness and cares of this life, and so that day come upon you unawares. For as a snare shall it come on all them that dwell on the face of the whole earth. Watch ye therefore, and *pray always,* that ye may be accounted worthy to escape all these things that shall come to pass, and to stand before the Son of man." According to this passage, there is only one way in which we can be prepared for the coming of the Lord when He appears: through much prayer.

The second coming of Jesus Christ is a subject that is awakening much interest and discussion in our day. It is one thing to be interested in the Lord's return and to talk about it, but it is quite another thing to be prepared for it. We live in an atmosphere that has a constant tendency to make us unsuitable for Christ's coming. The world tends to draw us down by its gratifications and cares. There is only one way by which we can triumphantly rise above these things—by constant watching in prayer, that is, by sleeplessness in prayer. *Watch* in this passage is the same strong word used in Ephesians 6:18, and *always* is the same strong phrase as pray at all times. The man who spends little time in prayer, who is not steadfast and constant in prayer, will not be ready for the Lord when He comes. But, we may be ready. How? Pray! Pray! Pray!

## We Need To Pray

*Because of what prayer accomplishes*.
Much has really been said about that already, but there is also much that should be added.

*Prayer promotes our spiritual growth* as almost nothing else, indeed, as nothing else except Bible study. True prayer and true Bible study go hand in hand.

It is through prayer that my sin is brought to

17

light, my most hidden sin. As I kneel before God and pray, "Search me, O God, and know my heart; try me, and know my thoughts: and see if there be any wicked way in me" (Psalm 139:23-24), God shoots the penetrating rays of His light into the innermost recesses of my heart. The sins I never suspected to be present are brought to light. In answer to prayer, God washes me from my iniquity and cleanses me from my sin (Psalm 51:2). In answer to prayer, my eyes are opened to behold wondrous things out of God's Word (Psalm 119:18). In answer to prayer, I receive wisdom to know God's way (James 1:5) and strength to walk in it. As I meet God in prayer and gaze into His face, I am changed into His image from glory to glory (2 Corinthians 3:18). Each day of true prayer life finds me more like my glorious Lord.

John Welch, the son-in-law of John Knox, was one of the most faithful men of prayer this world has ever seen. He counted any day in which seven or eight hours were not devoted solely to God in prayer and the study of His Word as wasted time. An old man speaking of him after his death said, "He was a type of Christ." How did he become so like his Master? His prayer life explains the mystery.

*Prayer also brings power into our work.* If we wish power for any work to which God calls us, be it preaching, teaching, personal work, or the raising of our children, we can receive it by earnest prayer.

A woman, with a little boy who was perfectly

incorrigible, once came to me in desperation and said: "What shall I do with him?"

I asked, "Have you ever tried prayer?"

She said that she had prayed for him, she thought. I asked if she had made his conversion and his character a matter of definite, expectant prayer. She replied that she had not been definite in the matter. She began that day, and at once there was a marked change in the child. As a result, he grew up into Christian manhood.

How many Sunday school teachers have taught for months and years and seen no real fruit from their labors. Then, they learn the secret of intercession and, by earnest pleading with God, see their students, one by one, brought to Christ! How many poor teachers have become mighty men of God by casting away their confidence in their own ability and gifts and giving themselves up to God to wait upon Him for the power that comes from on high! The evangelist John Livingstone spent a night, along with some believers, in prayer to God. When he preached the next day, five hundred people were either converted or marked some definite uplift in their spiritual life. Prayer and power are inseparable.

*Prayer avails for the conversion of others.* There are few converted in this world in any other way than in connection with someone's prayers. I previously thought that no human being had anything to do with my own conversion, for I was not converted in church or Sunday school or in personal conversation with anyone. I was awakened in the middle of the night and converted. As far as I can remember, I did not have the slightest thought of being converted, or of anything of that character, when I went to bed and fell asleep. But, I was awakened in the middle of the night and converted probably within five minutes. A few minutes before, I was about as near eternal damnation as one gets. I had one foot over the brink and was trying to get the other one over. As I said, I thought no human being had anything to do with it, but I had forgotten my mother's prayers. Later I learned that one of my college classmates had decided to pray for me until I was saved.

Prayer often avails where everything else fails. How utterly all of Monica's efforts and entreaties failed with her son! But, her prayers prevailed with God, and the immoral youth became St. Augustine, the mighty man of God. By prayer, the bitterest enemies of the gospel have become its most valiant defenders, the most wicked the truest sons of God, and the most contemptible women the purest saints. Oh, the power of prayer to reach down, where hope itself seems vain, and lift men and women up into fellowship with and likeness to God! It is simply wonderful! How little we appreciate this marvelous weapon!

*Prayer brings blessings to the Church.*

The history of the Church has always been full of grave difficulties to overcome. The devil hates the Church and seeks in every way to block its progress; by false doctrine, by division, and by inward corruption of life. But, by prayer, a clear way can be made through everything. Prayer will root out heresy, smooth out misunderstanding, sweep away jealousies and animosities, obliterate immoralities, and bring in the full tide of God's reviving grace. History abundantly proves this. In the darkest hour, when the state of the Church has seemed beyond hope, believing men and women have met together and cried to God, and the answer has come.

It was so in the days of Knox. It was so in the days of Wesley and Whitefield. It was so in the days of Edwards and Brainerd. It was so in the days of Finney. It was so in the days of the great revival of 1857 in this country and of 1859 in Ireland. And, it will be so again in your day and mine! Satan has organized his forces. Some people, claiming great apostolic methods, are merely covering the rankest dishonesty and hypocrisy with their loud and false assurance. Christians equally loyal to the great fundamental truths of the gospel are scowling at one another with a devil-sent suspicion. The world, the flesh, and the devil are holding a merry carnival. It is now a dark day, *but* now "it is time for Thee, Lord, to work: for they have made void Thy law" (Psalm 119:126). He is getting ready to work, and now He is listening for the voice of prayer. Will He hear it? Will He hear it from you? Will He hear it from the Church as a body? I believe He will.

## Chapter 2

## PRAYING TO GOD

After having seen some of the tremendous importance and resistless power of prayer, we now come directly to the lesson—how to pray with power.

In the twelfth chapter of Acts, we have the record of a prayer that prevailed with God and also brought about great results. In the fifth verse of this chapter, the manner and method of this prayer is described in a few words: "Prayer was made without ceasing of the church *unto God* for him" (Acts 12:5).

The first thing to notice in this verse is the brief expression "unto God." The prayer that has power is the prayer that is offered unto God.

But, some will say, "Is not all prayer offered unto God?"

No. Very much of so-called prayer, both public and private, is not unto God. In order for a prayer to really be unto God, there must be a definite and conscious approach to God when we pray. We must have a definite and vivid realization that God is bending over us and listening as we pray. In very much of our prayer, there is really only little thought of God. Our mind is taken up with the thought of what we need and is not occupied with the thought of the mighty and loving Father of whom we are seeking it. Oftentimes, we are neither occupied with the need nor with the One to whom we are praying. Instead, our mind is wandering here and there throughout the world. There is no power in that sort of prayer. But, when we really come into God's presence, really meet Him face to face in the place of prayer, really seek the things that we desire *from Him,* then there is power.

## Coming Into God's Presence

If we want to pray correctly, the first thing we should do is make sure that we really seek an audience with God—that we really get into His very presence. Before a word of petition is offered, we should have the definite and vivid consciousness that we are talking to God. Also, we should believe that He is listening to our petition and is going to grant the thing that we ask of Him. This is only possible by the Holy Spirit's power, so we should look to the Holy Spirit to really lead us into the presence of God. And, we should not be hasty in words until He has actually brought us there.

One night, a very active Christian man dropped into a little prayer meeting that I was leading. Before we knelt to pray, I said something like the above, telling all the friends to be sure, before they prayed, that they were really in God's presence. I also explained that while they were praying especially, they must have the thought of Him definitely in mind and be more taken up with Him than with their petition. A few days after I met this same gentleman, he said that this simple thought was entirely new to him. It had made prayer an entirely new experience to him.

If we want to pray correctly, these two little words must sink deep into our heart, *unto God*.

### Pray Without Ceasing

The second secret of effective praying is found in the same verse, in the words, *without ceasing*.

In the Revised Standard Version, "without ceasing" is rendered "earnest." Neither rendering gives the full force of the original Greek. The word literally means, "stretched-out-ed-ly." It is a pictorial word and wonderfully expressive. It represents the soul on a stretch of earnest and intense desire. "Intensely" would perhaps be as close a translation as any English word. It is the same word used to speak of our Lord in Luke 22:44, where it is said, "He prayed more earnestly: and His sweat was as it were great drops of blood falling down to the ground."

We read in Hebrews 5:7 that "in the days of His flesh" Christ "offered up prayers and supplications with strong crying and tears." In Romans 15:30, Paul begs the saints in Rome to *strive* together with him in their prayers. The word translated *strive* means primarily to contend as in athletic games or in a fight. In other words, the prayer which prevails with God is the prayer into which we put our whole soul, stretching out toward God in intense and agonizing desire. Much of our modern prayer lacks power because it lacks heart. We rush into God's presence, run through a string of petitions, jump up, and go out. If someone asks us an hour later what we prayed for, often we cannot remember. If we put so little heart into our prayers, we cannot expect God to put much heart into answering them.

We hear much in our day about the *rest* of faith, but there is no such thing as the *fight* of faith in prayer as there is in effort. Those who want us to think that they have attained to some great height of faith and trust because they have never known any agony of conflict or of prayer, have surely gotten beyond their Lord. They have even gone beyond the mightiest victors for God, both in effort and prayer, that the ages of Christian history have known. When we learn to come to God with an intensity of desire that wrings the soul, then we will know a power in prayer that most of us do not know now.

### Prayer And Fasting

How will we achieve this earnestness in prayer?

Not by trying to work ourselves up into it. The true method is explained in Romans 8:26: "Likewise the Spirit also helpeth our infirmities: for we know not what we should pray for as we ought: but the Spirit itself maketh intercession for us

26

with groanings which cannot be uttered." The earnestness that we work up in the energy of the flesh is a repulsive thing. The earnestness created in us by the Holy Spirit is pleasing to God. Here again, if we desire to pray correctly, we must look to the Spirit of God to teach us how to pray.

It is in this connection that fasting enters in. In Daniel 9:3, we read that Daniel set his face "unto the Lord God, to seek by prayer and supplications, with fasting, and sackcloth, and ashes." There are those who think that fasting belongs to the old dispensation. But, when we look at Acts 14:23 and Acts 13:2-3, we find that it was practiced by the earnest men of the apostolic day.

If we want to pray with power, we should pray with fasting. This of course does not mean that we should fast every time we pray. But, there are times of emergency or special crisis, when men of earnestness will withdraw themselves even from the gratification of natural appetites that would be perfectly proper under other circumstances, that they may give themselves up solely to prayer. There is a mysterious power in such prayer. Every great crisis in life and work should be met in that way. There is nothing pleasing to God in our giving up things which are pleasant in a purely Pharisaic and legal way. But, there is power in that downright earnestness and determination to obtain, in prayer, the things of which we strongly feel our need. This feeling of urgency leads us to put away everything, even things that are normal and necessary, that we may set our faces to find

God and obtain blessings from Him.

## Unity In Prayer

Another secret of proper praying is also found in this same verse, Acts 12:5. It appears in the three words, *of the church*.

There is power in *united prayer*. Of course, there is power in the prayer of an individual, but there is much more power in united prayer. God delights in the unity of His people and seeks to emphasize it in every way. Thus, He pronounces a special blessing upon united prayer. We read in Matthew 18:19, "If two of you shall agree on earth as touching any thing that they shall ask, it shall be done for them of My Father which is in heaven." This unity, however, must be real. The passage just quoted does not say that if two shall agree in asking, but if two shall agree *as touching* any thing they shall ask. Two persons might agree to ask for the same thing, and yet there may be no real agreement as touching the thing they asked. One might ask it because he really desired it, the other might ask it simply to please his friend. But, where there is real agreement, where the Spirit of God brings believers into perfect harmony concerning that which they ask of God, where the Spirit lays the same burden on two or more hearts, there is absolutely irresistible power in prayer.

Chapter 3

OBEYING AND PRAYING

One of the most significant verses in the Bible on prayer is 1 John 3:22. John says, "And whatsoever we ask, we receive of Him, because we keep His commandments and do those things that are pleasing in His sight."

What an astounding statement! John says, in so many words, that he received everything he asked for. How many of us can say this: "Whatsoever I ask I receive"? But, John explains why this was so, "Because we keep His commandments, and do those things that are pleasing in His sight." In other words, the one who expects God to do as he asks Him must *do whatever God bids him*. If we give a listening ear to all God's commands to us, He will give a listening ear to all our petitions to Him. If, on the other hand, we turn a deaf ear to His precepts, He will be likely to turn a deaf ear to our prayers. Here we find the secret of much unanswered prayer. We are not listening to God's Word, and, therefore, He is not listening to our petitions.

I was once speaking to a woman who had been a professed Christian but had given it all up. I asked her why she was not a Christian any longer. She replied, because she did not believe the Bible. I asked her why she did not believe the Bible.

"Because I have tried its promises and found them untrue."

"Which promises?"

"The promises about prayer."

"Which promises about prayer?"

"Does it not say in the Bible, 'Whatsoever ye ask believing ye shall receive?' "

"It says something nearly like that."

"Well, I asked fully expecting to get and did not receive, so the promise failed."

"Was the promise made to you?"

"Why, certainly, it is made to all Christians, is it not?"

"No, God carefully defines who the *ye's* are whose believing prayers He agrees to answer."

I then turned her to 1 John 3:22, and read the description of those whose prayers had power with God.

"Now," I said, "were you keeping His commandments and doing those things which are pleasing in His sight?"

She frankly confessed that she was not, and she soon came to see that the real difficulty was not with God's promises, but with herself. That is the reason for many unanswered prayers today: the one who offers them is not obedient.

## Knowing And Doing God's Will

If we want power in prayer, we must be earnest students of His Word to find out what His will regarding us is. Then having found it, we must do it. One unconfessed act of disobedience on our part will shut the ear of God against many petitions.

But, this verse goes beyond the mere keeping of God's commandments. John tells us that we must *do those things that are pleasing in His sight.*

There are many things which would please God, but which He has not specifically commanded. A true child is not content with merely doing those things which his father specifically commands him to do. He tries to know his father's will, and if he thinks that there is anything that he can do that would please his father, he does it gladly. He does so even if his father has never given him any specific order to do it. So it is with the true child of God. He does not merely ask whether certain things are commanded or certain things forbidden. He tries to know his Father's will in all things.

There are many Christians today who are doing things that are not pleasing to God. There are also many who neglect to do things which would be pleasing to God. When you speak to them about these things, they will confront you at once with the question, "Is there any command in the Bible not to do this thing?" If you cannot show them the verse in which their action is plainly forbidden, they think they are under no obligation whatever to give it up. But, a true child of God does not demand specific command. If we make it our desire to find out and do the things which are pleasing to God, He will make it His desire to do the things which are pleasing to us. Here again we find the explanation of much unanswered prayer. We are not making it our desire to know what pleases our Father. Thus, our prayers are not answered.

## Praying In Truth

Psalm 145:18 throws a great deal of light on the question of how to pray: "The Lord is nigh unto all them that call upon Him, to all that call upon Him in truth."

That little expression *in truth* is worthy of further study. If you take your concordance and go through the Bible, you will find that this expression means "in reality," "in sincerity." The prayer that God answers is the prayer that is real, the prayer that asks for something that is sincerely desired.

Much of our prayer is insincere. People ask for things which they do not wish. Many women pray for the conversion of their husbands, but do not really wish their husband to be converted. They think they do, but if they knew what would be involved in the conversion of their husbands, they would think again. It would necessitate an entire revolution in his manner of doing business and would consequently reduce their income, making it necessary to change their entire way of living. If they were sincere with God, the real prayer of their heart would be: "O God, do not convert my husband." Women do not wish their husbands' conversion at so great a cost.

Many churches are praying for a revival but do not really desire a revival. They think they do, for in their minds a revival means an increase of membership, of income, and of reputation among the churches. But, if they knew what a real revival meant, they would not be so eager. Revival brings the searching of hearts on the part of professed Christians, a radical transformation of individual, domestic, and social life, when the Spirit of God is poured out in reality and power. If all this were known, the real cry of the church would be: "O God, keep us from having a revival."

Many a minister is praying for the filling with the Holy Spirit, yet he does not really desire it. He thinks he does, for the filling with the Spirit means new joy and power in preaching the Word, a wider reputation among men, and a larger prominence in the Church of Christ. But, if he understood what a filling with the Holy Spirit really involved, he would think less about its rewards. He would think more of how it would necessarily bring him into antagonism with the world, with unspiritual Christians, how it would cause his name to be "cast out as evil," and how it might necessitate his leaving a good comfortable living and going down to work in the slums, or even in some foreign land. If he understood all this, his prayer most likely would be—if he were to express the real wish of his heart—"O God, save me from being filled with the Holy Spirit."

When we do come to the place where we really desire the conversion of friends at any cost, really desire the outpouring of the Holy Spirit whatever it may involve, really desire anything "in truth" and then call upon God for it "in truth," God is going to hear.

## Chapter 4

# PRAYING IN THE NAME OF CHRIST AND ACCORDING TO THE WILL OF GOD

It was a wonderful word about prayer that Jesus spoke to His disciples on the night before His crucifixion: "Whatsoever ye shall ask *in My name,* that will I do, that the Father may be glorified in the Son. If ye shall ask any thing in My name, I will do it" (John 14:13-14).

Prayer in the name of Christ has power with God. God is well pleased with His Son Jesus Christ. He always hears Him, and He also always hears the prayer that is really in His name. There is a fragrance in the name of Christ that makes every prayer that bears it acceptable to God.

But, what is it to pray in the name of Christ?

Many explanations have been attempted that make little sense to the average person. But, there is nothing mystical or mysterious about this expression. If you go through the Bible and examine all the passages in which the expression "in My name" or "in His name" are used, you will find that it means just about what it does in everyday language. If I go to a bank and hand in a check with my name signed to it, I ask of that bank *in my own name*. If I have money deposited in that bank, the check will be cashed; if not, it will not be. If, however, I go to a bank with somebody else's name signed to the check, I am asking *in his name*, and it does not matter whether I have money in that bank or any other. If the person whose name is signed to the check has money there, the check will be cashed.

If, for example, I were to go to the First National Bank of Chicago and present a check which I had signed for $50.00, the teller would say to me: "Why, Mr. Torrey, we cannot cash that. You have no money in this bank."

But, if I were to go to the First National Bank with a check for $50.00 made payable to me and signed by one of the large depositors in that bank, they would not ask whether I had money in that bank or in any bank. Instead, they would honor the check at once.

When I go to God in prayer, it is like going to the bank of heaven. I have nothing deposited there. I have absolutely no credit there. If I go in my own name, I will get absolutely nothing. But, Jesus Christ has unlimited credit in heaven, and He has granted me the privilege of going to the bank with His name on my checks. When I thus go, my prayers will be honored to any extent.

To pray in the name of Christ is to pray on the ground of His credit, not mine. It is to renounce the thought that I have any claims on God

whatever and approach Him on the ground of
Christ's claims. Praying in the name of Christ is
not done by merely adding the phrase, "I ask these
things in Jesus' name," to my prayer. I may put
that phrase in my prayer and really be resting in
my own merit all the time. On the other hand, I
may omit that phrase but really be resting in the
merit of Christ all the time. When I really do
approach God on the ground of Christ's merit and
His atoning blood (Hebrews 10:19), God will
hear me. Very much of our prayer is in vain
because men approach God imagining that they
have some claim on God which obligates Him to
answer their prayers.

### Forgiveness In His Name

Years ago when D. L. Moody was young in Christian work, he visited a town in Illinois. A judge in
the town was not a Christian. This judge's wife
asked Mr. Moody to call on her husband, but Mr.
Moody replied: "I cannot talk with your husband.
I am only an uneducated, young Christian, and
your husband is a scholarly non-believer."

But, the wife would not take *no* for an answer,
so Mr. Moody made the call. The clerks in the
outer office giggled as the young salesman from
Chicago went in to talk with the scholarly judge.

The conversation was short. Mr. Moody said:

"Judge, I can't talk with you. You are an educated non-Christian, and I have no learning. I simply want to say that if you are ever converted, I
want you to let me know."

The judge replied: "Yes, young man, if I am ever converted I will let you know. Yes, I will let you know."

The conversation ended. The clerks snickered even louder when the zealous, young Christian left the office, but the judge was converted within a year. Mr. Moody, visiting the town again, asked the judge to explain how it came about. The judge said:

"One night, when my wife was at prayer meeting, I began to grow very uneasy and miserable. I did not know what was the matter with me, but finally retired before my wife came home. I could not sleep all that night. I got up early, told my wife that I would eat no breakfast, and went down to the office. I told the clerks they could take a holiday and shut myself up in the inner office. I kept growing more and more miserable, and finally I got down and asked God to forgive my sins. But, I would not say, 'for Jesus' sake,' because I was a Unitarian and did not believe in the atonement. I kept praying, 'God forgive my sins,' but no answer came. At last, in desperation, I cried, 'O God, for Christ's sake forgive my sins,' and found peace at once."

The judge had no access to God until he came in the name of Christ. When he finally came in the name of Jesus, he was heard and answered at once.

### Knowing God's Will Through His Word

Great light is thrown upon the subject "How to Pray" by 1 John 5:14-15: "And this is the confi-

38

dence that we have in Him, that, if we ask any thing *according to His will,* He heareth us: and if we know that He hear us, whatsoever we ask, we know that we have the petitions that we desired of Him.''

This passage clearly teaches that if we are to pray correctly, we must pray according to God's will. Then, we will, beyond a shadow of a doubt, receive the thing we ask of Him.

But, can we know the will of God? Can we know that any specific prayer is according to His will?

We most surely can.

How?

First by the Word. God has revealed His will in His Word. When anything is definitely promised in the Word of God, we know that it is His will to give that thing. If, when I pray, I can find some definite promise of God's Word and lay that promise before God, I know that He hears me. And, if I know that He hears me, I know that I have the petition that I have asked of Him. For example, when I pray for wisdom. I know that it is the will of God to give me wisdom, for He says so in James 1:5: "If any of you lack wisdom, let him ask of God, that giveth to all men liberally, and upbraideth not; and it shall be given him." So, when I ask for wisdom, I know that the prayer is heard and that wisdom will be given me. In like manner, when I pray for the Holy Spirit I know from Luke 11:13 that it is God's will, that my prayer is heard, and that I have the petition that I have asked of Him. "If ye then, being evil, know how to give good gifts unto your children: how much more shall your heavenly Father give the Holy Spirit to them that ask Him?''

Some years ago, a minister came to me at the close of an address on prayer at a Y.M.C.A. Bible school and said, ''You have given those young men the impression that they can ask for definite things and get the very things that they ask.''

I replied that I did not know whether that was the impression I had given or not, but that was certainly the impression I desired to give.

''But,'' he replied, ''that is not right. We cannot be sure, for we don't know God's will.''

I turned at once to James 1:5, read it to him and said, ''Is it not God's will to give us wisdom, and if you ask for wisdom do you not know that you are going to get it?''

''Ah!'' he said, ''we don't know what wisdom is.''

I said, ''No, if we did, we would not need to ask. But, whatever wisdom may be, don't you know that you will get it?''

Certainly it is our privilege to know. When we have a specific promise in the Word of God, if we doubt that it is God's will or if we doubt that God will do that which we ask, we make God a liar.

Here is one of the greatest secrets of prevailing prayer: Study the Word to find what God's will is as revealed there in the promises. Then, simply take these promises and claim them before God in prayer with the absolutely unwavering expectation that He will do what He has promised in His

Word.

## Knowing God's Will By His Spirit

There is still another way in which we may
know the will of God—by the teaching of His
Holy Spirit. There are many things that we need
from God which are not covered by any specific
promise. But, we are not in ignorance of the will
of God even then. In Romans 8:26-27, we are told,
"Likewise the Spirit also helpeth our infirmities:
for we know not what we should pray for as we
ought: but the Spirit itself maketh intercession for
us with groanings which cannot be uttered; and
He that searcheth the hearts knoweth what is the
mind of the Spirit, because He maketh interession
for the saints *according to the will of God."* Here
we are distinctly told that the Spirit of God prays
in us, draws out our prayer, according to God's
will. When we are thus led out by the Holy Spirit
in any direction, to pray for any given object, we
may do it in all confidence that it is God's will. We
are to be assured that we will receive the very
thing we ask of Him, even though there is no specific promise to cover the case. Often, God by His
Spirit lays a heavy burden of prayer for some given
individual upon our heart. We cannot rest. We
pray for him with groanings which cannot be
uttered. Perhaps the man is entirely beyond our
reach, but God hears the prayer. And, in many
cases, it is not long before we hear of his definite
conversion.

The passage in 1 John 5:14-15 is one of the most

41

abused passages in the Bible: "This is *the confidence* that we have in Him, that, if we ask any thing according to His will, He heareth us: and if we know that He hear us, whatsoever we ask, we know that we have the petitions that we desired of Him." The Holy Spirit, without a doubt, put this passage into the Bible to encourage our faith. It begins with "this is *the confidence* that we have in Him," and closes with "*We know* that we have the petitions that we *desired of Him.*" But, one of the most frequent usages of this passage, which was so manifestly given to bring confidence, is to introduce an element of uncertainty into our prayers. Often, when a person is confident in prayer, some cautious brother will come and say:

"Now, don't be too confident. If it is God's will, He will do it. You should add, 'If it be Thy will.' "

Doubtless, there are many times when we do not know the will of God. And submission to the excellent will of God should be the basis for all prayer. But, when we know God's will, there need be no *if's*. This passage was not put into the Bible so that we could introduce *if's* into all our prayers, but so that we could throw our *if's* to the wind and have *"confidence"* and *"know* that we have the petitions which we have asked of Him."

## Chapter 5

# PRAYING IN THE SPIRIT

Over and over again in what has already been said, we have seen our dependence on the Holy Spirit in prayer. This is stated very clearly in Ephesians 6:18, "Praying always with all prayer and supplication *in the Spirit"*; and in Jude 20, "Praying *in the Holy Ghost."* Indeed, the whole secret of prayer is found in these three words, *in the Spirit*. God the Father answers the prayer that God the Holy Spirit inspires.

The disciples did not know how to pray as they should, so they came to Jesus and said, "Lord, teach us to pray." We also do not know how to pray as we should, but we have another Teacher and Guide right at hand to help us (see John 14:16-17). "The Spirit also helpeth our infirmities" (Romans 8:26). He teaches us how to pray. True prayer is prayer in the Spirit; that is, the prayer the Spirit inspires and directs. When we come into God's presence, we should recognize "our infirmities," our ignorance of what we should pray for or how we should pray for it. In the consciousness of our utter inability to pray properly, we should look up to the Holy Spirit, casting ourselves utterly upon Him to direct our prayers. He must lead our desires and guide our utterance of them.

Nothing can be more foolish in prayer than to rush heedlessly into God's presence and ask the first thing that comes into our mind. When we first come into God's presence, we should be silent before Him. We should look up to Him to send His Holy Spirit to teach us how to pray. We must wait for the Holy Spirit and surrender ourselves to the Spirit. Then, we will pray correctly.

Often, when we come to God in prayer, we do not feel like praying. What should we do in such a case? Cease praying until we feel like it? Not at all. When we feel least like praying is the time when we most need to pray. We should wait quietly before God and tell Him how cold and prayerless our hearts are. We should look up to Him, trust Him, and expect Him to send the Holy Spirit to warm our heart and draw us out in prayer. It will not be long before the glow of the Spirit's presence will fill our heart. We will begin to pray with freedom, directness, earnestness, and power. Many of the most blessed seasons of prayer I have ever known have begun with a feeling of utter deadness and prayerlessness. But, in my helplessness and coldness, I have cast myself upon God and looked to Him to send His Holy Spirit to teach me to pray. And, He has always done it.

When we pray in the Spirit, we will pray for the

right things in the right way. There will be joy and power in our prayer.

## Praying With Faith

If we are to pray with power, we must pray *with faith*. In Mark 11:24, Jesus says, "Therefore I say unto you, What things soever ye desire, when ye pray, believe that ye receive them, and ye shall have them." No matter how positive any promise of God's Word may be, we will not enjoy it unless we confidently expect its fulfillment. "If any of you lack wisdom," says James, "let him ask of God, that giveth to all men liberally, and upbraideth not; and it shall be given him" (James 1:5). Now, that promise is as positive as a promise can be. The next verse adds, "But let him ask in faith, nothing wavering. For he that wavereth is like a wave of the sea driven with the wind and tossed. For let not that man think that he shall receive any thing of the Lord" (James 1:6-7). There must then be confident, unwavering expectation. But, there is a faith that goes beyond expectation that believes that prayer is heard and the promise granted. This comes out in Mark 11:24, "Therefore I say unto you, What things soever ye pray, when ye pray, believe that ye receive them, and ye shall have them."

But, how can one have this faith?

Let us say with all emphasis, it cannot be forced. A person reads this promise about the prayer of faith and then asks for things that he desires. He tries to make himself believe that God has heard the prayer. This only ends in disappointment, for it is not real faith, and the thing is not granted. At this point, many people lose faith altogether by trying to create faith by an effort of their will. When the thing they made themselves believe they would receive is not given, the very foundation of faith is often undermined.

But, how does real faith come?

Romans 10:17 answers the question: "So then faith cometh by hearing, and hearing *by the Word of God.*" If we are to have real faith, we must study the Word of God and discover what is promised. Then, we must simply believe the promises of God. Faith must have God's sanction. Trying to believe something that you want to believe is not faith. Believing what God says in His Word is faith. If I am to have faith when I pray, I must find some promise in the Word of God to rest my faith on.

Faith furthermore comes through the Spirit. The Spirit knows the will of God. If I pray in the Spirit and look to the Spirit to teach me God's will, He will lead me out in prayer along the line of that will. He will give me faith that the prayer is to be answered. But, in no case does real faith come by simply determining that you are going to receive what you want. If there is no promise in the Word of God and no clear leading of the Spirit, there can be no real faith. There should be no scolding for your lack of faith in such a case. But, if the thing desired is promised in the Word of God, we may well scold ourselves for lack of faith if we doubt, for we are making God a liar by doubting His

Word.

## Chapter 6

## ALWAYS PRAYING AND NOT FAINTING

In the gospel of Luke, Jesus emphasizes the lesson that men ought to always pray and not faint. The first parable is found in Luke 11:5-8 and the other in Luke 18:1-8.

"And He said unto them, Which of you shall have a friend, and shall go unto him at midnight, and say unto him, Friend, lend me three loaves; For a friend of mine in his journey is come to me, and I have nothing to set before him? And he from within shall answer and say, Trouble me not: the door is now shut, and my children are with me in bed; I cannot rise and give thee. I say unto you, Though he will not rise and give him, because he is his friend, yet because of his importunity he will rise and give him as many as he needeth" (Luke 11:5-8).

"And He spake a parable unto them to this end, that men ought always to pray, and not to faint; Saying, There was in a city a judge, which feared not God, neither regarded man: And there was a widow in that city; and she came unto him, saying,

Avenge me of mine adversary. And he would not for a while: but afterward he said within himself, Though I fear not God, nor regard man; Yet because this widow troubleth me, I will avenge her, lest by her continual coming she weary me. And the Lord said, Hear what the unjust judge saith. And shall not God avenge His own elect, which cry day and night unto Him, though He bear long with them? I tell you that He will avenge them speedily. Nevertheless when the Son of man cometh, shall He find faith on the earth?'' (Luke 18:1-8).

In the former of these two parables, Jesus sets forth the necessity of importunity in prayer in a startling way. The word rendered *importunity* literally means *shamelessness*. Jesus wants us to understand that God desires us to draw nigh to Him with a determination to obtain the things we seek that will not be put to shame by any seeming refusal or delay on God's part. God delights in the holy boldness that will not take *no* for an answer. It is an expression of great faith, and nothing pleases God more than faith.

Jesus seemed to deal with the Syro-Phoenician woman almost with rudeness. But, she would not give up that easily, and Jesus looked upon her shameless persistance with pleasure. He said, ''O woman, great is thy faith: be it unto thee even as thou wilt'' (Matthew 15:28). God does not always give us things at our first effort. He wants to train us and make us strong by compelling us to work hard for the best things. Likewise, He does not always give us what we ask in answer to the first prayer. He wants to train us and make us strong people of prayer by compelling us to pray hard for the best things. He makes us *pray through*.

I am glad that this is so. There is no more blessed training in prayer than that which comes through being compelled to ask again and again, over long periods of time, before obtaining what we seek from God. Many people call it submission to the will of God when God does not grant them their requests at the first or second asking. They say, "Well, perhaps it is not God's will."

As a rule, this is not submission but spiritual laziness. We do not call it submission to the will of God when we give up after one or two efforts to obtain things by action. We call it lack of strength of character. When the strong man or woman of action starts out to accomplish a thing and does not accomplish it the first or second or one-hundredth time, he or she keeps hammering away until it is accomplished. The strong man of prayer keeps on praying until he prays it through and obtains what he seeks. We should be careful about what we ask from God. But, when we do begin to pray for a thing, we should never give up praying for it until we receive it or until God makes it very clear and very definite that it is not His will to give it.

Some people like us to believe that it shows unbelief to pray twice for the same thing. They think we ought to "take it" the first time we ask. Doubtless, there are times when we are able, through faith in the Word or the leading of the Holy Spirit, to *claim* the first time that which we have asked of God. But, beyond question, there are other times when we must pray again and again for the same thing before we receive our answer. Those who are beyond praying twice for the same thing are beyond their Master (Matthew 26:44). George Mueller prayed for two men daily for more than sixty years. One of these men was converted shortly before his death, I think at the last service that George Mueller held. The other was converted within a year after his death. One of the great needs of the present day is men and women who will not only start out to pray for things but pray on and on until they obtain what they seek from the Lord.

## Chapter 7

# ABIDING IN CHRIST

"If ye abide in Me, and My words abide in you, ye shall ask what ye will, and it shall be done unto you" (John 15:7). The whole secret of prayer is found in these words of our Lord. Here is prayer that has unbounded power: "Ask *what ye will, and it shall be done unto you.*"

There is a way then of asking and receiving precisely what we ask. Christ gives two conditions of this all-prevailing prayer:

The first condition is "If ye abide in *Me.*"

What is it to abide in Christ?

Some explanations are so mystical or so profound that many children of God think they mean practically nothing at all. But, what Jesus meant was really very simple.

He had been comparing Himself to a vine, His disciples to the branches in the vine. Some branches continued in the vine—in living union—so that the sap or life of the vine constantly flowed into the branches. They had no independent life of their own. Everything in them was simply the outcome of the life of the vine flowing into them. Their buds, leaves, blossoms, and fruit were not really theirs, but the buds, leaves, blossoms, and fruit of the vine. Other branches were completely severed from the vine, or the flow of the sap or life of the vine was in some way hindred. For us to abide in Christ is to bear the same relationship to Him that the first sort of branches bear to the vine. That is to say, to abide in Christ is to renounce any independent life of our own. We must give up trying to think our thoughts, form our resolutions or cultivate our feelings. We must simply and constantly look to Christ to think His thoughts in us, to form His purposes in us, to feel His emotions and affections in us. It is to renounce all life independent of Christ and constantly look to Him for the inflow of His life into us and the outworking of His life through us. When we do this, our prayers will obtain that which we seek from God.

This must necessarily be so, for our desires will not be our own desires but Christ's. And, our prayers will not in reality be our own prayers, but Christ praying in us. Such prayers will always be in harmony with God's will, and the Father always hears Him. When our prayers fail, it is because they are indeed our prayers. We have conceived the desire and offered our own petitions, instead of looking to Christ to pray through us.

To abide in Christ, one must already be in Christ through the acceptance of Christ as an atoning Savior from the guilt of sin. He must be acknowledged as a risen Savior from the power of sin and a Lord and Master over all the believer's life. Being in Christ, all that we have to do to abide (or continue) in Christ is simply to renounce our self-life. We must utterly renounce every thought, purpose, desire, and affection of our own and continually look for Jesus Christ to form His thoughts, purposes, affections, and desires in us. Abiding in Christ is really a very simple matter, though it is a wonderful life of privilege and of power.

### Christ's Words In Us

There is another condition stated in this verse, though it is really involved in the first: "And My words abide in you."

If we are to receive from God all we ask from Him, Christ's words must abide in us. We must study His words and let them sink into our thoughts and heart. We must keep them in our memory, obey them constantly in our life, and let them shape and mold our daily life and our every act.

This is really the method of abiding in Christ. It is through His words that Jesus imparts Himself to us. The words He speaks unto us, they are spirit and they are life (John 6:63). It is vain to expect power in prayer unless we meditate upon the words of Christ and let them sink deep and find a permanent abode in our hearts. There are many who wonder why they are so powerless in prayer. The very simple explanation of it all is found in their neglect of the words of Christ. They have not hidden His words in their hearts; His words do not abide in them. It is not by moments of mystical meditation and rapturous experiences that we learn to abide in Christ. It is by feeding upon His Word, His written word in the Bible, and looking to the Spirit to implant these words in our heart—to make them a living thing in our heart. If we thus let the words of Christ abide in us, they will stir us up to prayer. They will be the mold in which our prayers are shaped. And, our prayers will necessarily be along the line of God's will and will prevail with Him. Prevailing prayer is almost an impossibility where there is neglect of the study of God's Word.

Mere intellectual study of the Word of God is not enough; there must be meditation upon it. The Word of God must be revolved over and over in the mind with a constant looking to God and His Spirit to make that Word a living thing in the heart. The prayer that is born of meditation on the Word of God is the prayer which soars upward to God's listening ear.

George Mueller, one of the mightiest men of prayer, would begin praying by reading and meditating upon God's Word until a prayer began to form itself in his heart. Thus, God Himself was the real author of prayer, and God answered the prayer which He Himself had inspired.

The Word of God is the instrument through which the Holy Spirit works. It is the sword of the Spirit in more senses than one. The person who wants to know the work of the Holy Spirit in any direction must feed upon the Word. The person who desires to pray in the Spirit must meditate on the Word, so that the Holy Spirit may have something through which He can work. The Holy Spirit works His prayers in us through the Word. Neglect of the Word makes praying in the Holy Spirit an impossibility. If we seek to feed the fire of our prayers with the fuel of God's Word, all our difficulties in prayer will disappear.

Chapter 8

# PRAYING WITH THANKSGIVING

There are two words often overlooked in the lesson about prayer which Paul gives us in Philippians 4:6-7. "Be careful for nothing; but in every thing by prayer and supplication with thanksgiving let your requests be made known unto God. And the peace of God, which passeth all understanding, shall keep your hearts and minds through Christ Jesus." The two important words often overlooked are *with thanksgiving*.

In approaching God to ask for new blessings, we must never forget to thank Him for blessings already granted. If we would just stop and think about how many prayers God has answered, and how seldom we have thanked Him, I am sure we would be overwhelmed. We should be just as definite in returning thanks as we are in prayer. We come to God with very specific petitions, but when we thank Him our thanksgiving is indefinite and general.

Doubtless one reason why so many of our prayers lack power is because we have neglected

to thank God for blessings already received. If anyone were to constantly ask us for help and never
say, "Thank you" for the help given, we would
soon get tired of helping one so ungrateful.
Indeed, our respect for the one we were helping
would stop us from encouraging such rank ingratitude. Doubtless our heavenly Father, out of wise
regard for our highest welfare, often refuses to
answer our prayers in order to bring us to a sense
of our ingratitude. We must be taught to be thank-
ful.

God is deeply grieved by the thanklessness and
ingratitude of which so many of us are guilty.
When Jesus healed the ten lepers and only one
came back to give Him thanks, in wonderment and
pain, He exclaimed, "Were there not ten
cleansed? but where are the nine?" (Luke 17:17).

How often He looks down upon us in sadness at
our forgetfulness of His repeated blessings and frequent answers to prayer.

Returning thanks for blessings already received
increases our faith and enables us to approach
God with new boldness and new assurance.
Doubtless the reason so many have so little faith
when they pray is because they take so little time
to meditate upon and thank God for blessings
already received. As one meditates upon the
answers to prayers already granted, faith grows
bolder and bolder. We come to feel, in the very
depths of our soul, that there is nothing too hard
for the Lord. As we reflect on the wondrous good-
ness of God on the one hand and on the little

thanksgiving offered on the other hand, we may well humble ourselves before God and confess our sin.

The mighty men of prayer in the Bible, and those throughout the ages of the Church's history, have been men who were devoted to offering thanksgiving and praise. David was a mighty man of prayer, and his Psalms abound with thanksgiving and praise. The apostles were mighty men of prayer. We read that "they were continually in the temple, praising and blessing God" (Luke 24:53). Paul was a mighty man of prayer. Often in his epistles he bursts out in definite thanksgiving to God for definite blessings and definite answers to prayers. Jesus is our model in prayer as in everything else. In the study of His life, His manner of returning thanks at the simplest meal was so noticeable that two of His disciples recognized Him by this after His resurrection.

Thanksgiving is one of the inevitable results of being filled with the Holy Spirit. And, one who does not learn "in everything to give thanks" cannot continue to pray in the Spirit. If we want to learn to pray with power, we would do well to let these two words sink deep into our hearts: *"With thanksgiving."*

Chapter 9

# HINDRANCES TO PRAYER

We have very carefully studied the positive conditions of prevailing prayer. But, there are some things which hinder prayer. God has made these very plain in His Word.

## Selfish Prayers

The first hindrance to prayer is in James 4:3, "*Ye ask, and receive not, because ye ask amiss, that ye may consume it upon your lusts.*"

A selfish purpose in prayer robs prayer of power. Very many prayers are selfish. These may be prayers for things for which it is perfectly proper to ask, for things which it is the will of God to give. But, the motive of the prayer is entirely wrong, so the prayer falls powerless to the ground. The true purpose in prayer is that God may be glorified in the answer. If we ask any petition merely to receive something to use for our pleasure or gratification, we "ask amiss" and should not expect to receive what we ask. This explains why many prayers remain unanswered.

For example, a woman is praying for the conversion of her husband. That certainly is a most proper thing to ask. But, her motive in asking for the conversion of her husband is entirely improper; it is selfish. She desires that her husband may be converted because it would be so much more pleasant for her to have a husband who sympathized with her. Or, it is so painful to think that her husband might die and be lost forever. For some such selfish reason as this, she desires to have her husband converted. The prayer is purely selfish. Why should a woman desire the conversion of her husband? First and above all, that God may be glorified. It should be her desire because she cannot bear the thought that God the Father be dishonored by her husband.

Many pray for a revival. That certainly is a prayer that is pleasing to God—it is along the line of His will. But, many prayers for revivals are purely selfish. The churches desire revivals so that the membership may be increased or so that the church may have more power and influence in the community. Some churches want revival so that the church treasury may be filled or so that a good report may be made at the presbytery or conference or association. For such low purposes as these, churches and ministers are often praying for a revival. And, God does not answer the prayer. We should pray for a revival because we cannot endure the dishonor of God caused by the worldliness of the church, the sins of unbelievers, and the proud unbelief of the day. We should pray for revival because God's Word is being made void. We should pray for revival so that God may be glorified by the outpouring of His Spirit on the Church of Christ. For these reasons, first and above all, we should pray for a revival.

Many prayers for filling by the Holy Spirit are purely selfish prayers. It certainly is God's will to give the Holy Spirit to them that ask Him—He has told us so plainly in His Word (Luke 11:13). But, many prayers for filling by the Holy Spirit are hindered by the selfishness of the motive behind the prayer. Men and women pray for the Holy Spirit so that they may be happy, saved from the wretchedness of their lives, have power as Christian workers, or for some other purely selfish reason. We should pray for the Holy Spirit in order that God may no longer be dishonored by the low level of our Christian lives and by our ineffectual service. We should pray for the Holy Spirit so that God may be glorified in the new beauty that comes into our lives and the new power that comes into our service.

### Sin Hinders Prayer

The second hindrance to prayer is in Isaiah 59:1,2: "Behold, the Lord's hand is not shortened, that it cannot save. . . .But *your iniquities have separated between you and your God, and your sins have hid His face from you, that He will not hear.*"

Sin hinders prayer. Perhaps a man prays and prays and receives no answer to his prayer. Perhaps he is tempted to think that it is not the will of God to answer, or he may think that the days when God answered prayer are over. This is what the Israelites seem to have thought. They thought that the Lord's hand was shortened, that it could not save, and that His ear could no longer hear.

"Not so," said Isaiah, "God's ear is just as open to hear as ever, His hand just as mighty to save. But, there is a hindrance. That hindrance is your own sins. Your iniquities have separated you and your God. Your sins have hid His face from you that He will not hear."

It is likewise today. A man is crying to God in vain, simply because of sin in his life. It may be some sin in the past that has been unconfessed and unjudged. It may be some sin in the present that is cherished. Very likely it is not even looked upon as sin. But, the sin is there, hidden away somewhere in the heart or in the life, and God "will not hear."

Anyone who finds his prayers unanswered should not think that what he asks of God is not according to His will. Instead, he should go alone to God with the Psalmist's prayer, "Search me, O God, and know my heart: try me, and know my thoughts: and see if there be any wicked way in me" (Psalm 139:23-24). Wait before Him until He puts His finger upon the thing that is displeasing in His sight. Then, this sin should be confessed and put away.

I well remember a time in my life when I was praying for two definite things that I thought I must have, or God would be dishonored. But, the answer did not come. I awoke in the middle of the night in great physical suffering and great distress of soul. I cried to God for these things, reasoned with Him as to how necessary it was that I get them, and get them at once. Still no answer came. I asked God to show me if there was anything wrong in my own life. Something came to my mind that had often come to it before—something definite but which I was unwilling to confess as sin. I said to God, "If this is wrong, I will give it up." Still no answer came. In my innermost heart, though I had never admitted it, I knew it was wrong.

At last I said: "This is wrong. I have sinned. I will give it up."

I found peace. In a few moments I was sleeping like a child. In the morning, the money that was so much needed for the honor of God's name came.

Sin is an awful thing. One of the most awful things about it is the way it hinders prayer. It severs the connection between us and the source of all grace and power and blessing. Anyone who desires power in prayer must be merciless in dealing with his own sins. "If I regard iniquity in my heart, the Lord will not hear me" (Psalm 66:18). As long as we hold on to sin or have any controversy with God, we cannot expect Him to heed our prayers. If there is anything that is constantly coming up in your moments of close communion with God, that is the thing that hinders prayer. Put it away.

## Who Comes First?

The third hindrance to prayer is found in Ezekiel 14:3, "Son of man, these men have set up their idols in their heart, and put the stumbling-block of their iniquity before their face: should I be inquired of at all by them?" *Idols in the heart cause God to refuse to listen to our prayers*.

What is an idol? An idol is anything that takes the place of God, anything that is the supreme object of our affection. God alone has the right to the supreme place in our hearts. Everything and everyone else must be subordinate to Him.

Suppose a man makes an idol of his wife. Not that a man can love his wife too much, but he can put her in the wrong place. He can put her before God. When a man regards his wife's pleasure before God's pleasure, when he gives her the first place and God the second place, his wife is an idol. God cannot hear his prayers.

Suppose a woman makes an idol of her children. Not that we can love our children too much. The more dearly we love Christ, the more dearly we love our children. But, we can put our children in the wrong place, we can put them before God and their interests before God's interests. When we do this, our children are our idols.

Many men make an idol of their reputation or business. Reputation or business is put before God. God cannot hear the prayers of such men.

One great question for us to decide, if we really desire power in prayer, is, "Is God absolutely first?'' Is He before wife, before children, before reputation, before business, before our own lives? If not, prevailing prayer is impossible.

God often calls our attention to the fact that we have an idol by not answering our prayers. Thus, He leads us to inquire as to why our prayers are not answered. And so, we discover the idol, put it away, and God hears our prayers.

The fourth hindrance to prayer is found in Proverbs 21:13, *'' Whoso stoppeth his ears at the cry of the poor,* he also shall cry himself, but shall not be heard.''

### Give In Order To Receive

There is perhaps no greater hindrance to prayer than stinginess, the lack of generosity toward the poor and toward God's work. It is the one who gives generously to others who receives generously from God. ''Give, and it shall be given unto you; good measure, pressed down, and shaken together, and running over, shall men give into your bosom. For with the same measure that ye mete withal it shall be measured to you again'' (Luke 6:38). The generous man is the mighty man of prayer. The stingy man is the powerless man of prayer.

One of the most wonderful statements about prevailing prayer, 1 John 3:22, ''Whatsoever we ask we receive of Him, because we keep His commandments, and do those things that are pleasing in His sight,'' is made in direct connection with generosity toward the needy. In the context we are told it is when we love, not in word or in tongue, but in deed and in truth, when we open our hearts toward the brother in need that God hears us. It is then and only then we have confidence toward God in prayer.

Many men and women are seeking to find the secret of their powerlessness in prayer. They need not seek far. It is nothing more nor less than downright stinginess. George Mueller was a mighty man of prayer because he was a mighty giver. What he received from God never stuck to his fingers. He immediately passed it on to others. He was constantly receiving because he was constantly giving. When one thinks of the selfishness of the professing Church today, it is no wonder that the Church has so little power in prayer. If we want to receive from God, we must give to others. Perhaps the most wonderful promise in the Bible in regard to God's supplying our need is Philippians 4:19, "But my God shall supply all your need according to His riches in glory by Christ Jesus." This glorious promise was made to the Philippian church, and made in immediate connection with their generosity.

### An Unforgiving Spirit

The fifth hindrance to prayer is found in Mark 11:25, "And when ye stand praying, *forgive,* if ye have aught against any: that your Father also which is in heaven may forgive you your trespasses."

An unforgiving spirit is one of the most common hindrances to prayer. Prayer is answered on the basis that our sins are forgiven. However, God cannot deal with us on the basis of forgiveness while we are harboring ill will against those who have wronged us. Anyone who is nursing a grudge against another has closed the ear of God against his own petition. How many are crying to God for the conversion of husband, children, friends, and wondering why it is that their prayer is not answered. The whole secret to their dilemma is some grudge that they have in their hearts against someone who has injured them. Many mothers and fathers allow their children to go through to eternity unsaved for the miserable gratification of hating somebody.

## Husband And Wife Relationship

The sixth hindrance to prayer is found in 1 Peter 3:7, "Likewise, ye husbands, dwell with (your wives) according to knowledge, giving honour unto the wife, as unto the weaker vessel, and as being heirs together of the grace of life; that your prayers be not hindered." Here we are plainly told that *a wrong relationship between husband and wife is a hindrance to prayer*.

In many cases the prayers of husbands are hindered because of their failure of duty toward their wives. On the other hand, it is also doubtless true that the prayers of wives are hindered because of their failure in duty toward their husbands. If husbands and wives diligently seek to find the cause of their unanswered prayers, they will often find it in their relationship to one another.

Many men make great pretentions to holiness and are very active in Christian work but show little consideration in the treatment of their wives. It is often unkind, if not brutal. Then, they wonder why their prayers are not answered. The verse that we have just quoted explains the seeming mystery. On the other hand, many women are very devoted to the Church and very faithful in attendance yet treat their husbands with the most unpardonable neglect. They are cross and peevish toward them, and wound them by the sharpness of their speech and unruly temper. Then, they wonder why they have no power in prayer.

There are other things in the relationship between husbands and wives which cannot be spoken of publicly but which are often a hindrance in approaching God in prayer. There is much sin covered up under the holy name of marriage. This sin is a cause of spiritual deadness and of powerlessness in prayer. Any man or woman whose prayers seem to bring no answer should spread their whole married life out before God. They should ask Him to put His finger upon anything that is displeasing in His sight.

### Believe His Word Absolutely

The seventh hindrance to prayer is found in James 1:5-7, "But if any of you lack wisdom, let him ask of God, that giveth to all men liberally, and upbraideth not; and it shall be given him. But let him ask *in faith, nothing wavering*. For he that wavereth is like a wave of the sea driven with wind and tossed. For let not that man think that he shall receive any thing of the Lord."

Prayers are hindered by unbelief. God demands that we believe His Word absolutely. To question it is to make Him a liar. Many of us do that when we plead His promises. Is it any wonder that our prayers are not answered? How many prayers are hindered by our wretched unbelief! We go to God and ask Him for something that is positively promised in His Word, and then we only half expect to get it. "Let not that man think that he shall receive any thing of the Lord."

Chapter 10

# WHEN TO PRAY

If we want to know the fullness of blessing in the prayer life, it is important not only to pray in the right way but also at the right time. Christ's own example is full of suggestions as to the right time for prayer.

In the first chapter of Mark, verse 35, we read, "And *in the morning, rising up a great while before day,* He went out, and departed into a solitary place, and there prayed."

## Prayer In The Morning

*Jesus chose the early morning hour for prayer.* Many of the mightiest men of God have followed the Lord's example in this. In the morning hour the mind is fresh and at its very best. It is free from distraction. That absolute concentration which is essential to the most effective prayer is most easily possible in the early morning hours. Furthermore, when the early hours are spent in prayer, the whole day is sanctified. Power is then obtained for overcoming life's temptations and for performing its duties. More can be accomplished in prayer in the first hours of the day than at any other time during the day. Every child of God who wants to make the most out of his life for Christ should set apart the first part of the day to meet with God in the study of His Word and in prayer. The first thing we do each day should be to get alone with God. We can then face the duties, the temptations, and the service of that day, and receive strength from God for all. We should get victory before the hour of trial, temptation, or service comes. The secret place of prayer is the place to fight our battles and gain our victories.

## Nights Of Prayer

In the sixth chapter of Luke, verse 12, we find further light upon the right time to pray. We read, "And it came to pass in those days, that He went out into a mountain to pray, and continued *all night* in prayer to God."

Here we see Jesus praying in the night, spending the entire night in prayer. Of course, we have no reason to suppose that this was the constant practice of our Lord, nor do we even know how common this practice was. But, there were certainly times when the whole night was given up to prayer. Here, too, we do well to follow in the footsteps of the Master.

Of course, there is a way of setting apart nights for prayer in which there is no profit. It is pure legalism. But, the abuse of this practice is no reason for neglecting it altogether. One should not say, "I am going to spend a whole night in prayer," thinking that there is any merit that will win God's favor in such an exercise. That is legalism. But, we often do well to say, "I am going to set apart this night for meeting God and obtaining His blessing and power. If necessary, and if He so leads me, I will give the whole night to prayer." Often, we will have prayed things through long before the night has passed. Then we can retire and enjoy more refreshing and invigorating sleep than if we had not spent the time in prayer. At other times, God will keep us in communion with Himself way into the morning. When He does this in His infinite grace, blessed indeed are these hours of night prayer!

Nights of prayer to God are followed by days of power with men. In the night hours, the world is hushed in slumber. We can easily be alone with God and have undisturbed communion with Him. If we set apart the whole night for prayer, there will be no hurry. There will be time for our own hearts to become quiet before God. There will be time for the whole mind to be brought under the guidance of the Holy Spirit. There will be plenty of time to pray things through. A night of prayer should be put entirely under God's control. We should lay down no rules as to how long we will pray, or as to what we will pray about. Be ready to wait upon God for a short time or a long time as He may lead. Be ready to be led in one direction or another as He may see fit.

## Prayer Before And After A Crisis

Jesus Christ prayed *before all the great crises in His earthly life*.

He prayed before choosing the twelve disciples and before the Sermon on the Mount. He prayed before His anointing with the Holy Spirit and His entrance upon His public ministry. He prayed before announcing to the Twelve His approaching death and before the great consummation of His life on the cross. (See Luke 3:21,22; 6:12,13; 9:18,21,22; 22:39-46; Mark 1:35-38). He prepared for every important crisis by a lengthy season of prayer. We should do likewise. When any crisis of life is seen to be approaching, we should prepare for it by a season of very definite prayer to God. We should take plenty of time for this prayer.

Christ prayed not only before the great events and victories of His life, but He also prayed *after its great achievements and important crises* .

When He had fed the five thousand with the five loaves and two fishes, the multitude desired to take Him and make Him king. Having sent them away, He went up into the mountain to pray and spent hours there alone with God (Matthew 14:23; John 6:15). So He went on from victory to victory.

It is more common for most of us to pray before the great events of life than it is to pray after them. But, the latter is as important as the former. If we prayed after the great achievements of life, we might go on to still greater. As it is, we are often either exalted or exhausted by the things that we do in the name of the Lord, and so we advance no further. Often, a man, in answer to pray, has been endued with power and has thus worked great things in the name of the Lord. When these great things were accomplished, instead of going alone with God and humbling himself before Him—giving Him all the glory—he has congratulated himself. He has become arrogant, and God has been obliged to lay him aside. The great things done were not followed by humiliation of self and prayer to God. Thus, pride has come in, and the mighty man has been stripped of his power.

## Never Too Busy

Jesus Christ gave special time to prayer *when life was unusually busy*. He would withdraw from the multitudes that thronged about Him and go into the wilderness to pray. For example, we read in Luke 5:15-16, "But so much the more went there a fame abroad of Him: and great multitudes came together to hear, and to be healed by Him of their infirmities. And He withdrew Himself into the wilderness and prayed."

Some men are so busy that they find no time for prayer. Apparently, the busier Christ's life was, the more He prayed. Sometimes He had no time to eat (Mark 3:20). Sometimes He had no time for needed rest and sleep (Mark 6:31,33,46). But, He always took time to pray. The more the work increased, the more He prayed.

Many mighty men of God have learned this secret from Christ. And, when the work has increased more than usual, they have set an unusual amount of time apart for prayer. Other men of God, once mighty, have lost their power because they did not learn this secret. They allowed increasing work to crowd out prayer.

Years ago, it was my privilege, with other theological students, to ask questions of one of the most useful, Christian men of the day. I was led to ask, "Will you tell us something of your prayer life?"

The man was silent a moment, and then, turning his eyes earnestly upon me, replied: "Well, I must admit that I have been so swamped with work lately that I have not given the time I should to prayer."

Is it any wonder that man lost power. The great work he was doing was curtailed in a very marked degree. Let us never forget that the more the work presses on us, the more time we must spend in prayer.

### Pray At All Times

Jesus Christ prayed *before the great temptations of His life*.

As He drew nearer and nearer to the cross and realized that the great final test of His life was imminent, Jesus went out into the garden to pray. He came "unto a place called Gethsemane, and saith unto the disciples, Sit ye here, while I go and pray yonder" (Matthew 26:36). The victory of

Calvary was won that night in the garden of Gethsemane. The calm majesty with which He bore the awful onslaughts of Pilate's Judgment Hall and Calvary resulted from the struggle, agony, and victory of Gethsemane. While Jesus prayed, the disciples slept. He stood fast while they fell dishonorably.

Many temptations come upon us suddenly and unannounced. All that we can do is lift a cry to God for help then and there. But, many temptations of life we can see ahead of time, and, in such cases, the victory should be won before the temptation really reaches us.

In 1 Thessalonians 5:17 we read, "Pray *without ceasing*," and in Ephesians 6:18, "Praying *at all times*."

Our whole life should be a life of prayer. We should walk in constant communion with God. There should be a constant looking upward to God. We should walk so habitually in His presence that even when we awake in the night it would be the most natural thing for us to speak to Him in thanksgiving or petition.

Chapter 11

# THE NEED OF A GENERAL REVIVAL

If we are to pray correctly in such a time as this, much of our prayer should be for a general revival. If there was ever a need to cry unto God in the words of the Psalmist, "Wilt Thou not revive us again: that Thy people may rejoice in Thee?" (Psalm 85:6), it is this day in which we live. It is surely time for the Lord to work, for men have made void His law. The voice of the Lord given in the written Word is made void both by the world and the Church. Such a time is not a time for discouragement—the man who believes in God and the Bible can never be discouraged. But, it is a time for Jehovah Himself to step in and work. The intelligent Christian, the alert watchman on the walls of Zion, may well cry with the Psalmist, "It is time for Thee, Lord, to work: for they have made void Thy law" (Psalm 119:126).

The great need of the day is a general revival. Let us consider first of all what a general revival is.

A revival is a time of quickening or impartation of life. As God alone can give life, a revival is a

time when God visits His people. By the power of
His Spirit, He imparts new life to them. Through
them, He imparts life to sinners dead in trespasses
and sins. We have spiritual enthusiasm contrived
by the cunning methods and hypnotic influence of
the mere professional evangelist. But, these are
not revivals and are not needed. They are the
devil's imitations of a revival. *New life from
God*—that is a revival. A general revival is a time
when this new life from God is not confined to
scattered localities. It is general throughout Chris-
tendom and the earth.

The reason why a general revival is needed is
that spiritual desolation and death is general. It is
not confined to any one country, though it may be
more manifest in some countries than in others. It
is found in foreign mission fields as well as in
home fields. We have had local revivals. The life-
giving Spirit of God has breathed on this minister
and that, this church and that, this community and
that. But, we sorely need a widespread and general
revival.

Let us look, for a few moments, at the results of
a revival. These results are apparent in ministers of
the Church and in the unsaved.

### Revival In Ministers

The results of a revival in ministers are:

*The ministers have a new love for souls.* We
ministers, as a rule, have no such love for souls as
we ought to have. We have no such love for souls
as Jesus had or as Paul had. But, when God visits

His people, the hearts of ministers are greatly burdened for the unsaved. They go out in great longing for the salvation of their fellow-men. They forget their ambition to preach great sermons and for fame, and simply long to see men brought to Christ.

*The ministers receive a new love for and faith in God's Word.*They cast off their doubts and criticisms of the Bible and start preaching the Bible and, especially, Christ crucified. Revivals make ministers, who are loose in their doctrines, orthodox. A genuine, widesweeping revival would do more to set things right than all the heresy trials ever instituted.

*Revivals bring to ministers new liberty and power in preaching.*It is no week-long grind to prepare a sermon, and no nerve-consuming effort to preach it after it has been prepared. Preaching is a joy and refreshment. There is power in it during times of revival.

### Revival In Christians

The results of a revival in Christians generally are as noticeable as as its results upon the ministry.

*In times of revival, Christians come out from the world and live separated lives.* Christians who have been amused with the world and its pleasures give them up. These things are found to be incompatible with increasing life and light.

*In times of revival, Christians receive a new spirit of prayer.* Prayer meetings are no longer a duty but become the necessity of a hungry, persistant heart. Private prayer is followed with new zest. The voice of earnest prayer to God is heard day and night. People no longer ask, "Does God answer prayer?" They know He does, and they besiege the throne of grace day and night.

*In times of revival, Christians go to work for lost souls.* They do not go to meetings simply to enjoy themselves and get blessed. They go to meetings to watch for souls and to bring them to Christ. They talk to men on the street and in the stores and in their homes. The cross of Christ, salvation, heaven, and hell become the subjects of constant conversation. Politics, the weather, new fashions, and the latest novels are forgotten.

*In times of revival, Christians have new joy in Christ.* Life is joy, and new life is new joy. Revival days are glad days, days of heaven on earth.

*In times of revival, Christians receive a new love for the Word of God.* They want to study it day and night. Revivals are bad for taverns and theaters, but they are good for bookstores and Bible publishers.

### Revival's Influence On The Unsaved

Revivals also have a decided influence on the unsaved world.

First of all, they bring deep conviction of sin. Jesus said that when the Spirit was come He would convince the world of sin (John 16:7,8). Now, we have seen that a revival is a coming of the Holy Spirit. Therefore, there must be a new conviction of sin, and there always is. If you see something which men call a revival and there is no conviction of sin, you may know immediately that it is false. It is a sure sign.

Revivals also bring conversion and regeneration. When God refreshes His people, He always converts sinners as well. The first result of Pentecost was new life and power to the one hundred and twenty disciples in the upper room. The second result was three thousand conversions in a single day. It is always so. I am constantly reading of revivals where Christians were greatly encouraged but there were no conversions. I have my doubts about that kind of revival. If Christians are truly refreshed, they will get after the unsaved by prayer and testimony and persuasion. And, there *will* be conversions.

## Why General Revival Is Needed

We know what a general revival is and what it does. Let us now face the question why it is needed at the present time.

I think that the mere description of what it is and what it does shows that it is sorely needed. Let us look at some specific conditions that exist today that show the need of it. In showing these conditions, one is likely to be called a pessimist. If facing the facts is pessimistic, I am willing to be a pessimist. If in order to be an optimist one must shut his eyes and call black white, error truth, sin righteousness, and death life, I don't want to be an optimist. But, I am an optimist all the same. Pointing out the real condition will lead to a better condition.

Look again at the ministry.

Many of us who profess to be orthodox ministers are practically non-believers. That is plain speech, but it is also indisputable fact. There is no essential difference between the teachings of the liberal Tom Paine and the teachings of some of our theological professors. The latter are not so blunt and honest about it. They phrase it in more elegant and studied sentences. But, it means the same. Much of the so-called new learning and higher criticism is simply Tom Paine's infidelity sugar-coated. A German professor once read a statement of some positions, then asked if they fairly represented the scholarly criticism of the day. When it was agreed that they did, he startled his audience by saying: "I am reading from Tom Paine's *Age of Reason.*"

There is little new in the higher criticism. Our future ministers often are being educated under immoral professors. Being immature men when they enter college or the seminary, they naturally come out non-believers in many cases. Then, they go forth to poison the Church.

Even when our ministers are orthodox—as, thank God, so very many are—they are often not men of prayer. How many modern ministers know what it is to wrestle in prayer, to spend a good share of a night in prayer? I do not know how many, but I do know that many do not.

Many of us who are ministers have no love for souls. How many preach because they *must* preach? How many preach because they feel that men everywhere are perishing, and by preaching they hope to save some? And, how many follow up their preaching, as Paul did, by beseeching men everywhere to be reconciled to God?

Perhaps enough has been said about us ministers. But, it is evident that a revival is needed for our sake. If not, some of us will have to stand before God overwhelmed with confusion in an awful day of reckoning that is surely coming.

Look now at the *doctrinal state of the Church*. It is bad enough. Many do not believe in the whole Bible. The book of Genesis is a myth, Jonah is an allegory, and even the miracles of the Son of God are questioned. The doctrine of prayer is old-fashioned, and the work of the Holy Spirit is sneered at. Conversion is unnecessary, and hell is no longer believed in. Look at the fads and errors which have sprung up out of this loss of faith. Christian Science, Unitarianism, Spiritualism, Universalism, Metaphysical Healing, etc., etc., a perfect pandemonium of the doctrines of devils.

Look at the *spiritual state of the Church*. Worldliness is rampant among church members. Many church members are just as eager as any to become rich. They use the methods of the world in the accumulation of wealth. And, they hold on to it just as tightly once they have gotten it.

Prayerlessness abounds among church members on every hand. Someone has said that Christians, on the average, do not spend more than five minutes a day in prayer.

Neglect of the Word of God goes hand in hand with neglect of prayer to God. Many Christians spend twice as much time everyday engrossed in the daily papers as they do bathing in the cleansing Word of God. How many Christians average an hour a day in Bible study?

Along with neglect of prayer and the Word of God goes a lack of generosity. The churches are rapidly increasing in wealth, but the treasuries of the missionary societies are empty. Christians do not average a dollar a year for foreign missions. It is simply appalling.

Then, there is the increasing disregard for the Lord's Day. It is fast becoming a day of worldly pleasure, instead of a day of holy service. The Sunday newspaper with its mundane rambling and scandal has replaced the Bible. Visiting, golfing, and bicycling have replaced Sunday school and the church service.

Christians mingle with the world in all forms of questionable amusements. The young man or young woman who does not believe in wearing immodest clothing, participating in wild parties, and attending the theater with its ever-increasing appeal to lewdness is considered an old fogey.

How small a proportion of our membership has really entered into fellowship with Jesus Christ in His burden for souls! Enough has been said of the spiritual state of the Church.

Now look at the *state of the world*.

Note how few conversions there are. Here and there a church has a large number of new members joining by confession of faith, but these churches are rare. Where there are such new members, in very few cases are the conversions deep, thorough, and satisfactory.

There is lack of conviction of sin. Seldom are men overwhelmed with a sense of their awful guilt in dishonoring the Son of God. Sin is regarded as a "misfortune," "infirmity," or even as "good in the making." Seldom is it considered an enormous wrong against a holy God.

Unbelief is rampant. Many regard it as a mark of intellectual superiority to reject the Bible as well as faith in God and immortality. It is often the only mark of intellectual superiority many possess. Perhaps that is the reason they cling to it so dearly.

Hand in hand with this widespread atheism goes gross immorality, as has always been the case. Atheism and immorality are Siamese twins. They always exist and increase together. This prevailing immorality is found everywhere.

Look at the legalized adultery that we call divorce. Men marry one wife after another and are still admitted into good society; and women do likewise. There are thousands of supposedly respectable men in America living with other men's wives. And, there are thousands of supposedly respectable women living with other women's husbands.

This immorality is found in much modern theater. Many questionable characters of the stage rule the day. And, the individuals who degrade themselves by appearing in such off-color plays are defended in the newspapers and welcomed by supposedly respectable people.

Much of our literature is rotten, but decent people will read bad books because it is the rage. Art is often a mere covering for shameless indecency. Women are induced to cast modesty to the wind that the artist may perfect his art and defile his morals.

Greed for money has become an obsession with rich and poor. The multimillionaire will often sell his soul and trample the rights of his fellow-men in the hope of becoming a billionaire. The working man will often commit murder to increase the power of the union and keep up wages. Wars are waged and men shot down like dogs to improve commerce and to gain political prestige for unprincipled politicians who parade as statesmen.

The licentiousness of the day lifts its serpent head everywhere. You see it in the newspapers, on the billboards, in advertisements for cigars, shoes, bicycles, medicines, and everything else. You see it on the streets at night. You see it just outside the church door. You find it in the awful ghettos set apart for it in great cities. And, it is crowding further and further up our business streets and into the residential portions of our cities. Alas! Every so often you find it, if you look closely, in supposedly respectable homes. Indeed it will be borne to your ears by the confessions of brokenhearted men and women. The moral condition of the world is disgusting, sickening, and appalling.

## Pray For Revival

We need a revival—deep, widespread, general—in the power of the Holy Spirit. It is either a general revival or the dissolution of the Church, of the home, and of the state. A revival, new life from God, is the cure—the only cure. Revival will halt the awful tide of immorality and unbelief. Mere argument will not do it. But, a wind from heaven, a new outpouring of the Holy Spirit, a true God-sent revival will. Atheism, higher criticism, Christian Science, Spiritualism, Universalism, all will go down before the outpouring of the Spirit of God. It was not discussion but the breath of God that banished non-believers of old to the limbo of forgetfulness. And, we need a new breath from God to send the current, radical non-Christians to keep those non-believers of old company. I believe that breath from God is coming.

The great need of today is a general revival. The need is clear. It allows no honest difference of opinion. What then must we do? Pray. Take up the Psalmist's prayer, "Revive us again: that Thy people may rejoice in Thee" (Psalm 85:6). Take up Ezekiel's prayer, "Come from the four winds. O breath (breath of God), and breathe upon these slain, that they may live" (Ezekiel 37:9). Hark, I hear a noise! Behold a shaking! I can almost feel the breeze upon my cheek. I can almost see the great living army rising to their feet. Will we not pray and pray and pray and pray until the Spirit comes, and God revives His people?

Chapter 12

# PRAYER BEFORE AND DURING REVIVALS

No treatment of the subject "How to Pray" would be at all complete if it did not consider the place of prayer in revivals.

The first great revival of Christian history had its origin on the human side in a ten-day prayer meeting. We read of that handful of disciples, "These all continued with one accord in prayer and supplication" (Acts 1:14). The result of that prayer meeting is in the second chapter of the Acts of the Apostles, "They were all filled with the Holy Ghost, and began to speak with other tongues, as the Spirit gave them utterance" (verse 4). Further on in the chapter, we read that "there were added unto them about three thousand souls" (verse 41). This revival proved genuine and permanent. The converts "continued steadfastly in the apostles' doctrine and fellowship, and in breaking of bread, and in prayers" (Acts 2:42). "And the Lord added to the church daily such as should be saved" (Acts 2:47).

## Testimonies Of Answered Prayer

Every true revival from that day to this has had its earthly origin in prayer. The great revival under Jonathan Edwards in the eighteenth century began with his famous call to prayer. The marvelous work of grace among the Indians under Brainerd began in the days and nights that he spent before God in prayer for an enduement of power from on high for this work.

A most remarkable and widespread display of God's reviving power was the revival in Rochester, New York, in 1830, under the labors of Charles G. Finney. It not only spread throughout the state but ultimately to Great Britain as well. Mr. Finney himself attributed the power of this work to the spirit of prayer that prevailed. He describes it in his autobiography in the following words:

"When I was on my way to Rochester, as we passed through a village, some thirty miles east of Rochester, a brother minister whom I knew, seeing me on the canal-boat, jumped aboard to have a little conversation with me, intending to ride but a little way and return. He, however, became interested in conversation, and upon finding where I was going, he made up his mind to keep on and go with me to Rochester. We had been there but a few days when this minister became so convicted that he could not help weeping aloud at one time as we passed along the street. The Lord gave him a powerful spirit of prayer, and his heart was broken. As he and I prayed together, I was struck with his faith in regard to what the Lord was going to do there. I recollect he would say, 'Lord, I do not know how it is; but I seem to know that Thou art going to do a great work in this city.' The spirit of prayer was poured out powerfully, so much so that some persons stayed away from the public services to pray, being unable to restrain their feelings under preaching.

"And here I must introduce the name of a man, whom I shall have occasion to mention frequently, Mr. Abel Clary. He was the son of a very excellent man, and an elder of the church where I was converted. He was converted in the same revival in which I was. He had been licensed to preach; but his spirit of prayer was such, he was so burdened with the souls of men, that he was not able to preach much, his whole time and strength being given to prayer. The burden of his soul would frequently be so great that he was unable to stand, and he would writhe and groan in agony. I was well acquainted with him, and knew something of the wonderful spirit of prayer that was upon him. He was a very silent man, as almost all are who have that powerful spirit of prayer.

"The first I knew of his being in Rochester, a gentleman who lived about a mile west of the city, called on me one day and asked me if I knew a Mr. Abel Clary, a minister. I told him that I knew him well.

" 'Well,' he said, 'he is at my house, and has been there for some time, and I don't know what to think of him.'

"I said, 'I have not seen him at any of our meetings.'

" 'No,' he replied, 'he cannot go to meetings, he says. He prays nearly all the time, day and night, and in such agony of mind that I do not know what to make of it. Sometimes he cannot even stand on his knees, but will lie prostrate on the floor, and groan and pray in a manner that quite astonishes me.'

"I said to the brother, 'I understand it: please keep still. It will come out right; he will surely prevail.'

"I knew at the time a considerable number of men who were exercised in the same way. . . .This Mr. Clary and many others among the men, and a large number of women partook of the same spirit, and spent a great part of their time in prayer. Father Nash, as we called him who in several of my fields of labor came to me and aided me, was another of those men that had such a powerful spirit of prevailing prayer. This Mr. Clary continued in Rochester as long as I did, and did not leave it until after I had left. He never, that I could learn, appeared in public, but gave himself wholly to prayer.

"I think it was the second Sabbath that I was at Auburn at this time, I observed in the congregation the solemn face of Mr. Clary. He looked as if he was borne down with an agony of prayer. Being well acquainted with him, and knowing the great gift of God that was upon him, the spirit of prayer, I was very glad to see him there. He sat in the pew with his brother, the doctor, who was also a professor of religion, but who had nothing by experience, I should think, of his brother Abel's great power with God.

"At intermission, as soon as I came down from the pulpit, Mr. Clary, with his brother, met me at the pulpit stairs, and the doctor invited me to go home with him and spend the intermission and get some refreshments. I did so.

"After arriving at his house we were soon summoned to the dinner table. We gathered about the table, and Dr. Clary turned to his brother and said, 'Brother Abel, will you ask the blessing?' Brother Abel bowed his head and began, audibly, to ask a blessing. He had uttered but a sentence or two when he broke instantly down, moved suddenly back from the table, and fled to his chamber. The doctor supposed he had been taken suddenly ill, and rose up and followed him. In a few moments he came down and said, 'Mr. Finney, Brother Abel wants to see you.'

"Said I, 'What ails him?'

"Said he, 'I do not know but he says you know. He appears in great distress, but I think it is the state of his mind.'

"I understood it in a moment, and went to his room. He lay groaning upon the bed, the Spirit making intercession for him, and in him, with groanings that could not be uttered. I had barely entered the room, when he made out to say, 'Pray, Brother Finney.' I knelt down and helped him in prayer, by leading his soul out for the conversion of sinners. I continued to pray until his distress passed away, and then I returned to the dinner table.

"I understood that this was the voice of God. I saw the Spirit of prayer was upon him, and I felt His influence upon myself, and took it for granted that the work would move on powerfully. It did so. The pastor told me afterward that he found that in the six weeks that I was there, five hundred souls had been converted."

## Persistent Prayer Results

Mr. Finney in his lectures on revivals tells of other remarkable awakenings in answer to the prayers of God's people. He says in one place, "A clergyman. . .told me of a revival among his people, which commenced with a zealous and devoted woman in the church. She became anxious about sinners, and went to praying for them; she prayed, and her distress increased; and she finally came to her minister, and talked with him, and asked him to appoint an anxious meeting, for she felt that one was needed. The minister put her off, for he felt nothing of it. The next week she came again, and besought him to appoint an anxious meeting; she knew there would be somebody to come, for she felt as if God was going to pour out His Spirit. He put her off again. And finally she said to him, 'If you do not appoint an anxious meeting I shall die, for there is certainly going to be a revival.' The next Sabbath he appointed a meeting, and said that if there were any who wished to converse with him about the salvation of their souls, he would meet them on such an evening. He did not know of one, but when he went to the place, to his astonishment he found a large number of anxious inquirers.''

In still another place he says, ''The first ray of light that broke in upon the midnight which rested on the churches in Oneida county, in the fall of 1825, was from a woman in feeble health, who, I believe had never been in a powerful revival. Her soul was exercised about sinners. She was in agony for the land. She did not know what ailed her, but she kept praying more and more, till it seemed as if her agony would destroy her body. At length she became full of joy and exclaimed, 'God has come! God has come! There is no mistake about it, the work is begun, and is going over all the region!' And sure enough, the work began, and her family was almost all converted, and the work spread all over that part of the country.''

The great revival of 1857 in the United States began in prayer and was carried on by prayer more than by anything else. Dr. Cuyler in an article in a religious newspaper some years ago said, ''Most revivals have humble beginnings, and the fire starts in a few warm hearts. Never despise the day of small things. During all my own long ministry, nearly every work of grace has a similar beginning. One commenced in a meeting gathered at a few hours' notice in a private house. Another commenced in a group gathered for Bible study by Mr. Moody in our mission chapel. Still another—the most powerful of all—was kindled on a bitter January evening at a meeting of young Christians under my roof. That profound Christian, Dr. Thomas H. Skinner of the Union Theological Seminary, once gave me an account of a remarkable coming together of three earnest men in his study when he was the pastor of the Arch Street Church in Philadelphia. They literally wrestled in prayer. They made a clean breast in confession of sin, and humbled themselves before God. One and another church officer came in and joined them. The Heaven-kindled flame soon spread through the whole congregation in one of the most powerful revivals ever known in that city.''

## Prayer Knows No Boundaries

In the early part of the sixteenth century, there was a great religious awakening in Ulster, Ireland. The lands of the rebel chiefs, which had been forfeited to the British crown, were settled by a class of colonists who were governed by a spirit of wild adventure. Authentic righteousness was rare. Seven ministers, five from Scotland and two from England, settled in that country, the earliest arrivals being in 1613. A contemporary of one of these ministers named Blair recorded: "He spent many days and nights in prayer, alone and with others, and was vouchsafed great intimacy with God." Mr. James Glendenning, a man of very meager natural gifts, was a man similarly minded in regard to prayer. The work began under this man Glendenning. The historian of the time says, "He was a man who never would have been chosen by a wise assembly of ministers, nor sent to begin a reformation in this land. Yet this was the Lord's choice to begin with him the admirable work of God which I mention on purpose that all may see how the glory is only the Lord's in making a holy nation in this profane land, and that it was 'not by might, nor by power, but by My Spirit, saith the Lord of hosts' (Zechariah 4:6)." In his preaching at Oldstone, multitudes of hearers felt great anxiety and terror of conscience. They looked on themselves as altogether lost and damned and cried out, "Men and women, what will we do to be saved?" They were stricken by the power of His Word. In one day a dozen were carried out of doors as dead. These were not cowards, but some of the boldest spirits of the neighborhood; "some who had formerly feared not with their swords to put a whole market town into a fray." Concerning one of them, the historian writes, "I have heard one of them, then a mighty strong man, now a mighty Christian, say that his end in coming into church was to consult with his companions how to work some mischief."

This work spread throughout the whole country of Ireland. By the year 1626, a monthly concert of prayer was held in Antrim. The work spread beyond the bounds of Down and Antrim to the churches of the neighboring counties. The spiritual interest became so great that Christians would come thirty or forty miles to the communions. They would continue from the time they came until they returned without wearying or making use of sleep. Many of them neither ate nor drank, and yet some of them professed that they "went away most fresh and vigorous, their souls so filled with the sense of God."

This revival changed the whole character of northern Ireland.

Another great awakening in Ireland in 1859 had a somewhat similar origin. By many who were unaware, it was thought that this marvelous work came without warning and preparation. But, Rev. William Gibson, moderator of the General Assembly of the Presbyterian Church in Ireland in 1860, in his history of the awakening, tells how there had been two years of preparation. There had been constant discussion in the General Assembly of the low state of spiritual fervor and the need of a revival. There had been special sessions for prayer. Finally, four young men, who became leaders in the origin of the great work, began to meet together in an old schoolhouse. Around the spring of 1858, a work of power began to manifest itself. It spread from town to town, from county to county. The congregations became too large for the buildings, and the meetings were held in the open air. They were often attended by many thousands of people. Many hundreds of people were frequently convicted of sin in a single meeting. In some places, the criminal courts and jails were closed for lack of occupation. There were manifestations of the Holy Spirit's power of a most remarkable character. This clearly proves that the

Holy Spirit is as ready to work today as in apostolic days. He will do so when ministers and Christians really believe in Him and begin to prepare the way by prayer.

Mr. Moody's wonderful work in England and Scotland and Ireland, then afterwards in America, originated in prayer. Mr. Moody made little impression until men and women began to cry to God. Indeed, his going to England at all was in answer to the persistant cries to God by a bedridden saint. While the spirit of prayer continued, the revival grew in strength. But, in the course of time, less and less was made of prayer, and the work fell off in power. One of the great secrets of the superficiality and unreality of many of our modern, so-called revivals is that more dependence is put on man's machinery than on God's power. His power must be sought and obtained by earnest, persistent, believing prayer. We live in a day characterized by the multiplication of man's machinery and the decrease of God's power. The great cry of our day is work, new organizations, new methods, new machinery. The great need of our day is prayer.

## Church—Wake Up!

It was a master stroke of Satan when he got the Church to so generally lay aside this mighty weapon of prayer. Satan is perfectly willing that the Church multiply its organizations and contrive machinery for the conquest of the world for Christ if it will only give up praying. He laughs as he looks at the Church today and says to himself,

"You can have your Sunday schools and your Young People's Societies. Enjoy your Young Men's Christian Associations and your Women's Christian Temperance Unions. Continue your Institutional Churches, your Industrial Schools, and your Boys' Brigades. Worship with your grand choirs, your fine organs, your brilliant preachers, and your revival efforts, too. But, don't bring the power of Almighty God into them by earnest, persistent, believing, mighty prayer."

Prayer could work as marvelously today as it ever could, if the Church would only take up the call.

There seems to be increasing signs that the Church is awaking to this fact. Here and there God is laying a burden of prayer upon individual ministers and churches like they have never known before. Less dependence is being placed on machinery and more on God. Ministers are crying to God day and night for power. Churches and groups are meeting together in the early morning hours and the late night hours crying to God for the latter rain. There is every indication of the coming of a mighty and widespread revival. There is every reason why, if a revival should come in any country at this time, it should be more widespread in its extent than any revival of history. There is the closest and swiftest communication by satellite, air waves, and cable between all parts of the world. A true fire of God kindled in America would soon spread to the uttermost parts of the earth. The only thing needed to bring this fire is prayer.

It is not necessary that the whole Church begin praying at first. Great revivals always begin in the hearts of a few men and women whom God arouses by His Spirit to believe in Him as a living God. They believe He is a God who answers prayer. Upon their heart He lays a burden from which no rest can be found except in persistant crying unto God.

May God use this book to arouse many others to pray so that the greatly-needed revival may come, and come quickly.

Let Us Pray!